Supplement to *British Book News*: No. 23

THOMAS CARLYLE

By DAVID GASCOYNE

PUBLISHED FOR
THE BRITISH COUNCIL
and the NATIONAL BOOK LEAGUE
by LONGMANS, GREEN & CO.
LONDON. NEW YORK. TORONTO

Revised Price
2s. 6d. net

The re-discovery or re-interpretation of the greater figures of the Victorian age proceeds apace. Ruskin has lately attracted scholarship and good writing, and in this essay Mr. David Gascoyne shows reason why Thomas Carlyle should be considered by contemporaries as of the first importance. Although he is remembered largely by *The French Revolution* (1837) and by his great edition of *Oliver Cromwell's Letters and Speeches* (1845) it is rather as a prophet, and as a commentator on his own times, that Mr. Gascoyne finds him significant and exciting.

Mr. Gascoyne, now in his middle thirties, published his first book of poems, *Roman Balcony*; a novel, *Opening Day*; and *A Short History of Surrealism*, while still in his teens. His later poems, and in particular his volume, *A Vagrant* (1950) shows the continuance of that early brilliance. He has also published translations of the work of André Breton, Péret, and Hölderlin, and he brings to the study of Carlyle a wide knowledge of European literature.

Bibliographical Series
of *Supplements to* 'British Book News'

★

GENERAL EDITOR
T. O. Beachcroft

THOMAS CARLYLE
from a painting by J. A. McN. WHISTLER *in the Art Gallery of the Corporation of Glasgow.*

THOMAS CARLYLE

By DAVID GASCOYNE

PUBLISHED FOR
THE BRITISH COUNCIL
and the NATIONAL BOOK LEAGUE
BY LONGMANS, GREEN & CO., LONDON, NEW YORK, TORONTO

LONGMANS, GREEN & CO. LTD.
6 & 7 Clifford Street, London, W.1
Also at Melbourne and Cape Town

LONGMANS, GREEN & CO. INC.
55 Fifth Avenue, New York, 3

LONGMANS, GREEN & CO.
215 Victoria Street, Toronto, 1

ORIENT LONGMANS LTD.
Bombay, Calcutta, Madras

First published in 1952

PR
4433
.G22

*Printed in Great Britain by Benham and Company Limited
Colchester*

CONTENTS

THOMAS CARLYLE *page* 7

A SELECT BIBLIOGRAPHY 33

INDEX OF ESSAYS AND PAPERS 40

THOMAS CARLYLE on a midnight ramble in Chelsea, 1859. From a pen-and-ink drawing by C. B. Birch in the National Portrait Gallery.

¶ THOMAS CARLYLE was born at Ecclefechan in Annandale, Scotland, on 4 December 1795. He died on 4 February 1881 and was buried in his native place.

THOMAS CARLYLE

Just as the individual man may aspire to become something, so does the age; and this is what it aspires to : it would build up the established order, abolish God, and through fear of men cow the individual into a mouse's hole—but this is what God will not have, and He employs the exactly opposite tactics : He employs the individual to provoke the established order out of its self-complacency.

SØREN KIERKEGAARD
—*Training in Christianity*

In January 1836, two years after first taking up residence in Cheyne Row in Chelsea, Thomas Carlyle wrote in his *Journal*:

I thought to-day up at Hyde Park Corner, seeing all the carriages dash hither and thither, and so many human bipeds cheerily hurrying along, ' There you go, brothers, in your gilt carriages and prosperities, better or worse, and make an extreme bother and confusion, the devil very largely in it. And I too, by the blessing of the Maker of me, I too am authorized and equipped by Heaven's Act of Parliament to do that small secret somewhat, and will do it without any consultation of yours. Let us be brothers, therefore, or at most silent peaceable neighbours, and each go his own way.

He went his way, and did indeed accomplish his secret somewhat; and at this distance it appears to be anything but small. Now his statue is to be found on the Chelsea Embankment; and at Westminster, almost as much a monument to Carlyle as to the only Christian dictator known to History, outside the House of Commons, stands the statue of the man whom Carlyle succeeded in persuading Englishmen to reconsider and duly to honour, Oliver Cromwell.

From early manhood to old age, Carlyle was aware of a vocation, a duty, and responsibility : to bear witness to the Divine nature of the true man, and to speak and write the Truth as far as it lay in him to do so, and thus to transmit the message of God to man in his generation. To the sophisticated modern reader, this will seem an odd and outmoded solemn way of speaking; but unless one realizes that this was indeed how Carlyle himself conceived his life's task, and that it is to just this exceptional seriousness that his writing owes its strength, one will not be likely to form anything like a just estimate of Carlyle's importance. If there is anything that ought more than another thing to be said at present, half-way through the twentieth century, about the importance of Carlyle, it is that he is more than a great Victorian writer, he is one of our great national prophets, and as such, a writer whose message is still full of import to living men and women. For the time being, his situation is much the same as that of another great Victorian prose writer, Ruskin; if either of them is referred to, it is often for the purpose of drawing attention to the pitiable or distasteful nature of his character and private life; what interests modern critics seems to be far less what they had to say than the unsuccessful nature of their marriages.

The ideal unread Carlyle of to-day, the popular image of him, that is to say, by which his reality is hidden from most people at present, is a dyspeptic, irascible old man in a dressing-gown, an egoist alternately cruel and indifferent to his too clever wife, and an early prophet of Fascism and the cult of the Superman.

Instead of attempting an argued refutation of such unverisimilitude, let me quote a remark made by Leigh Hunt, who for many years was a close neighbour of the Carlyles: 'I believe that what Mr. Carlyle loves better than his fault-finding, with all its eloquence, is the face of any human creature that looks suffering and loving and sincere'; which is not the sort of thing that is likely to be said about any man unless there is very good reason for it. Elizabeth Barrett Browning, in a letter to a friend written in 1851, said of Carlyle: 'It is difficult to conceive of a more interesting human soul, I think. All the bitterness is love with the point reversed.' And another revealing couple of sentences are two of his own, from a letter to his wife written after a period of stomach and domestic trouble (two kinds of trouble which really were practically synonymous for Carlyle) : ' Nay, to tell you the truth, your anger at me ... was itself sometimes a kind of comfort to me. I thought, "Well, she has strength enough to be cross and ill-natured at me ; she is not all softness and affection and weakness ".'

The fact, which must be mentioned before I proceed further, that there are *two Carlyles*, has been the subject of a distinguished book of criticism by Mr. Osbert Burdett ; and I say the fact advisedly, for it seems to me that this is not a matter merely of one critic's speculative theory. There are two Carlyles almost as indubitably as there are two Hegels, two Wordsworths. What factor should be pointed to as having been most responsible for the transition from the first to the second, it is a delicate matter to decide, as this transition cannot be precisely dated. London, which was irresistible to him, and which he could never leave for long after the move from Scotland in 1834, did something to him, no doubt, and something more than weary, exasperate, and sadden him. His own eventual success may have done something to him, besides intensifying his sense of the hypocrisy of Britain in the Crystal Palace Age. His mind did not grow weaker, but much sorrow seems to have benumbed it ; and perhaps, after all, much though the determining influence on his work of his digestive and nervous systems has been exaggerated by journalists, it was the Fiend Dyspepsia that finally eroded the keen edge of his thought, and led him to resort increasingly often to the reiteration of his own formulae. Before leaving the subject, one can but ask whether the influence on Carlyle's life of his friendship with Lady Harriet Baring, or rather, with the Ashburtons, since Lord Ashburton, Lady Harriet's husband, remained also his close friend until his death, may not have had something to do with the change. The Seer of Craigenputtock and the Sage of Chelsea, though one and the same man, are not, whatever it was that transformed the one into the other, one and the same thinker ; nor can it be said that half a lifetime's experience of life in the British capital, not without many encounters with *le beau monde*, contributed any notable addition to the Sage's wisdom.

Carlyle's first important book, one of the most astonishing first books by any author of genius of the nineteenth century, was entirely conceived and written on his native heath. And in *Sartor Resartus* we may find as disillusioned a picture of the true nature of early Victorian society—in the chapter in which an Irish family meal, and an English aristocrat's (or parvenu's ? this is not specified) toilet, are shown us in contrasting tableaux as illustrative of the vast yawning chasm that at that time separated the social extremes—as any of the lurid cartoons to be found in the *Latter-Day Pamphlets* or later writings. There crept into his later analyses of what was wrong with society at least one fundamental error that vitiates a good deal of what he had to say on this subject during the second half of his life: the quasi-Manichean notion of a God who loves 'good citizens' and detests criminals.

Thomas Carlyle was one of the sternest critics of the nineteenth century's special pride, the rise and progress of Democracy, yet he himself was one of the most striking examples of a kind of triumph which is thought to be one of Democracy's chief justifications. The son of a Scots house-builder and contractor, of simple working-class family, Carlyle early in young manhood became the translator and personal friend of undisputably the greatest and most influential man in Europe, Goethe; and in his old age Queen Victoria sought to make his acquaintance as having himself become one of the most influential great men of her reign. In his early life he and his wife lived in what were then called 'the most straitened of circumstances'; before he died his writings, not one of which was ever influenced by the least monetary consideration, had made him a wealthy independent man, able to contribute anonymously to many philanthropic causes. His life is an irreproachable example of the achievement of the Hero as Man of Letters.

Before he died, Carlyle had already become the Grand Old Man of Victorian Literature, the 'Sage of Chelsea', and it is this figure of him, as represented in the famous Whistler portrait, that has remained in the popular imagination ever since. One of the ways in which the reading public protects itself from dynamic influences is that of prematurely canonizing the disturbing genius, and circulating a picturesque legend about him accompanied by some poster-like pictorial image and an easily memorized cliché, slogan, or quotation. Acquaintance with this superficial epitome-effigy dispenses one from the effort of reading the collected works of the writer thus represented, whose living essence from then on is hidden from view and becomes less and less known to posterity.

One of the most frequently repeated of modern misunderstandings of Carlyle is the idea that, because he was a critic of Democracy and an admirer of Heroes, he must have been one of the thinkers who prepared the way for Totalitarianism, along with Houston Stewart Chamberlain and the Comte de Gobineau. This is a disgraceful misunderstanding, and could only have grown so common in a society which had ceased to know any longer what it means to *believe* in anything higher than self-interest and the necessity for compromise. It is one of the many prevalent mild forms of insanity to believe that one's critics are always one's enemies. If what they say is true, they are on the contrary one's best friends. What Carlyle loathed and detested, and denounced so fervidly, was not the Democracy we know now that we really do want to achieve and perpetuate, but the early nineteenth century misconception masquerading under that name. If the last hundred years have witnessed a very considerable transformation in the popular understanding of what is meant by Democracy, and at least it is certain that no one to-day really believes that it means *laissez-faire*, then Carlyle is certainly one of the writers whom we have to thank most for the change.

The thing that Carlyle had to tell the society of his time was that it had departed from Truth and Sincerity, and that the materialist ideal of profit and prosperity which, with the newly-laid-down railways and the ever more triumphant progress of industrial development on every hand, was whirling everyone away towards a future of entirely delusory glory, was a base and ungodly ideal. How vehemently and how repetitively he said just this, and in what accents of tremendous, reverberative denunciation and admonition !

Unhappy Workers, unhappier Idlers, unhappy men and women of this actual England. We are yet very far from an answer, and there will be no existence for us without finding one. "A fair day's-wages for a fair day's-work :" it is as just a demand as Governed men ever made of Governing. It is the everlasting right of man. Indisputable as Gospels, as arithmetical multiplication-tables : it must and will have itself fulfilled ;—and yet, in these times of ours, with what enormous difficulty, next-door to impossiblity !

For the times are really strange ; of a complexity intricate with all the new width of the ever widening world ; times here of half-frantic velocity of impetus, there of the deadest-looking stillness and paralysis ; times definable as showing two qualities, Dilettantism and Mammonism ; most intricate obstructed times ! Nay, if there were not a Heaven's radiance of Justice, prophetic, clearly of Heaven, discernible behind all these confused world-wide entanglements, of Landlord interests, Manufacturing interests, Tory-Whig interests, and who knows what other interests, expediencies, vested interests, established possessions, inveterate Dilettantisms, Midas-eared Mammonisms—it would seem to every one a flat impossibility, which all wise men might as well at once abandon. If you do not know eternal Justice from momentary Expediency, and understand in your heart of hearts how Justice, radiant, beneficent, as the all-victorious light-element, is also in essence, if need be, an all-victorious *Fire*-element, and melts all manner of vested interests, and the hardest iron cannon, as if they were soft wax, and does ever in the long-run rule and reign, and allows nothing else to rule and reign—you also would talk of impossibility ! But it is only difficult, it is not impossible. Possible ? It is, with whatever difficulty, very clearly inevitable.

(*Past and Present*, Bk. I, Chap. 3)

When I described Carlyle as a great 'national prophet', I was not using the term in any loose sense. Three of Carlyle's books are entirely devoted to a kind of writing that is very exactly to be described as prophetic. In *Chartism* (published in 1840), in *Past and Present* (1843) and the *Latter-Day Pamphlets* (1850), Carlyle addresses the British nation and presents a vision of History, an exposure of the reality underlying present appearances and an evocation of the collective Future, at once terrible and yet to the eye of faith wonderfully hopeful. All three books are written in a prose that has much, except metre, in common with poetry, and rising in many passages to a dythyrambic pitch. With the exception of certain books of Ruskin's, particularly *Unto this Last* (1862), there is nothing else in Victorian prose literature comparable to these works. Among general works of literature of the nineteenth century, only a few, such as Whitman's *Democratic Vistas*, Kierkegaard's *The Present Age* and *Attack on 'Christendom'*, certain pages of Baudelaire's prose, certain portions of Nietzsche's writing, may be said to belong to the same sort of category.

To-day it would seem more difficult than ever to understand immediately what Carlyle meant by the term Hero. During the last twenty-five years the world has witnessed such a huge preposterous travesty of the Heroic idea and had such a ghastly revelation of the true nature of Humbug-heroism in the rise and fall of the Nazi and Fascist movements that one would have thought men would not be likely to fall a-worshipping any sort of Hero again for a long while to come. But large numbers of the world's population apparently feel no shame in bowing the knee to dictators of wide diversity; and I hardly dare assert of so large a number of people that they all ought to be blushing.

As long as one refrains from actually reading with care *On Heroes, Hero-Worship and the Heroic in History* it is easy to remain convinced that the subject is one most suited to adolescence. After reading the book, it is still possible to feel that Carlyle's conception is a little confusing and does not seem to have been firmly grounded on a clear preliminary definition. Plenty of definitions are thrown out during the course of the six lectures, but there is nothing to indicate a recognition of the fact that Heroism is essentially a matter of narrative, not of a man's feats or character. Men do not become Heroes during their own lifetime; or if they do, seldom survive the transient adoration of their contemporaries, certainly not if they themselves seek for or approve of it. Carlyle himself failed to recognize Abraham Lincoln as the one man among his contemporaries who might truly be thought worthy to be described as a man of the same mould as the Lord Protector of our former Commonwealth.

The six lectures on Heroes were first delivered in May 1840. If since then they had been read as often as they have been referred to, we should no doubt have heard a great deal less about Carlyle the prophet of Fascism. The epithet is far less appropriate to him than it is even to Nietzsche. To begin with, it is quite clearly the Divine Right of Kings that modern dictators have attempted to reappropriate to themselves, and Carlyle's favourite hero, it should constantly be remembered, was *not* Charles I, but the common man who was forced by his Puritan conscience to assume national leadership in defence of civil liberty *against* autocracy. None of Carlyle's heroes (unless it be Napoleon, about whom his enthusiasm is but lukewarm) bears the slightest resemblance to any twentieth-century national political figure, with the possible exception of Mr. Winston Churchill. As all honest thinking people must have realized long ago, the ideology of Fascism is completely without intellectual integrity, and its ideals are pompous imitations; and the Democracies, in refusing any longer to recognize the usurped authority of the Dictators and allying themselves with all men in Europe who revolted against their tyrannous regime, were actually assuming the heroic responsibility of resisting Falsehood and taking up arms in the defence of Truth, or rather of the faith that Truth exists. The Democracy that Carlyle attacked with such bitterness and pertinacity no longer existed in the Europe of the 1930's except in those countries where the worship of Shams had become compulsory.

The book cannot, I think, be regarded as by any means one of Carlyle's best, though after *The French Revolution* it is probably the most famous. It is unwearyingly repetitive and uninterruptedly exhortative and picturesque, and it must be admitted that its manner may make it a little difficult to assimiliate much more than half a hero at a time. While on the subject of Carlyle's style, however, I think I should say that the modern reader is just as likely as a Victorian to find it fascinating, and a most exhilarating change from the blandly correct or casual manner of nine out of ten modern authors; or on the other hand, to find it exasperating, a portentous rumbling and intolerable bore. In my opinion, the reader who finds himself in the latter case is to be pitied; but I will say no more on this subject, which since Carlyle first appeared in print, has occasioned more than enough inept, quite styleless comment.

As Cromwell may be said to have been Carlyle's favourite Hero, Boswell may be cited as an example of his idea of the Hero-worshipper. A good deal of the following passage from his concluding lecture, on Johnson, might be thought to apply to-day almost equally well to Carlyle himself:

> Johnson's Writings, which once had such currency and celebrity, are now, as it were, disowned by the young generation. It is not wonderful; Johnson's opinions are fast becoming obsolete: but his style of thinking and of living, we may hope, will never become obsolete. I find in Johnson's Books the indisputablest traces of a great intellect and great heart: —ever welcome, under what obstructions and perversions soever. They are *sincere* words, those of his; he means things by them. A wondrous buckram style,—the best he could get to then; a measured grandiloquence, stepping or rather stalking along in a very solemn way, grown obsolete now; sometimes a tumid *size* of phraseology not in proportion to the contents of it: all

this you will put-up with. For the phraseology, tumid or not, has always *something within it*. So many beautiful styles and books with *nothing* in them ;—a man is a *male*factor to the world who writes such ! *They* are the avoidable kind !

It will perhaps be only fair to let Carlyle himself have the last word on the subject of his lectures *On Heroes and Hero-Worship*. This is what he noted in his *Journal* after the last of the series had been delivered :

> Jane says, and indeed I rather think it is true, that these last two lectures are among the best I ever gave (she says the very best, but I do not think that) ; and certainly they have not done me nearly so much mischief as the others were wont. I feel great pain and anxiety till I get them done on the day when they are to be done ; but no excessive shattering of myself to pieces in consequence of that.
>
> I got through the last lecture yesterday in very tolerable style, seemingly much to the satisfaction of all parties ; and the people all expressed in a great variety of ways much very genuine-looking friendliness for me. I contrived to tell them something about poor Cromwell, and I think to convince them that he was a great and true man, the valiant soldier in England of what John Knox had preached in Scotland. In a word, the people seemed agreed that it was my best course of lectures, this. And now you see I am handsomely through it, and ought to be very thankful.

The three principal prophetic books of Carlyle are not the books of his most likely to attract the modern reader ; and it is doubtful whether they are read to-day except by specializing students. This is a pity, for they all contain magnificent pages of writing, and are not wholly limited to the discussion of mid-Victorian problems. The title of the first, and the shortest, of these books, *Chartism* (1840), suggests that its interest is wholly early Victorian ; and this may account for the fact that surprisingly few people seem to be acquainted with the magnificent vision and epitome of English history that it contains, a piece of writing only fifteen pages in length which would seem one of the most essential texts in all Victorian literature for the purposes of a national democratic Education.

When *Past and Present* first appeared in 1843, Emerson, in reviewing the book in *The Dial* called it ' Carlyle's new poem, his *Iliad* of English woes, to follow his poem on France, entitled the *History of the French Revolution* . . . it is a political tract, and since Burke, since Milton, we have had nothing to compare with it '. This monumental rhapsody of Gothic prose built in four parts—' Proem ', ' The Ancient Monk ', ' The Modern Worker ', ' Horoscope '—is a series of rotatory ruminations on this theme (essentially the same as that ' God is Dead ! ' which is the theme of much of Nietzsche's) : Man among the dark Satanic mills of Industrialism has lost his Soul, modern society is no longer bound together by the cement of living faith, human life devoid of spirit is only death and sordid nightmare !

> It is even so. To speak in the ancient dialect, we ' have forgotten God ' ; in the most modern dialect and very truth of the matter, we have taken up the Fact of the Universe as it is *not*. We have quietly closed our eyes to the eternal Substance of things, and opened them only to the Shows and Shams of things. . . .
> (*Past and Present*, Bk. III, Chap. 1)

This was the state of affairs he had already described in his previous book, *Chartism* :

> Alas, in such times it grows to be the universal belief, sole accredited knowingness, and the contrary of it accounted puerile enthusiasm, this sorrowfulest *dis*belief that there is properly speaking any truth in the world ; that the world ever has been or ever can be guided, except by simulation, dissimilation, and the sufficiently dextrous practice of pretence. The faith of men is dead : in what has guineas in its pocket, beef-eaters riding behind it, and cannons trundling before it, they can believe ; in what has none of these things they cannot believe. Sense for the true and false is lost ; there is properly no longer any true or false. It is the heyday of Imposture ; of Semblance recognising itself, and getting itself recognised, for

Substance. Gaping multitudes listen; unlistening multitudes see not but that all is right, and in the order of Nature. Earnest men, one of a million, shut their lips; suppressing thoughts, which there are no words to utter. To them it is too visible that spiritual life has departed; that material life, in whatsoever figure of it, cannot long remain behind. . . .
(Chartism, Chap. 5)

Such is the state of affairs into which the writer who may be called prophet is sent. His function is to diagnose and understand the spiritual malady of the age, and to interpret the age to itself, by articulating, and not shutting his lips from, the thoughts which other earnest men suppress or leave unuttered. And the core and essence of his message is this : ' that Speciosities which are not Realities cannot any longer inhabit this world.'

Alas, was that such new tidings? Is it not from of old indubitable, that Untruth, Injustice which is but acted untruth, has no power to continue in this true Universe of ours? The tidings was world-old, as old as the Fall of Lucifer: and yet in that epoch unhappily it was new tidings, unexpected, incredible; and there had to be such earthquakes and shakings of the nations before it could be listened to, and laid to heart even slightly! Let us lay it to heart, let us know it well, that new shakings be not needed. Known and laid to heart it must everywhere be, before peace can pretend to come. This seems to us the secret of our convulsed era; this which is so easily written, which is and has been and will be so hard to bring to pass. All true men, high and low, each in his sphere, are consciously or unconsciously bringing it to pass; all false and half-true men are fruitlessly spending themselves to hinder it from coming to pass.
(Chartism, Chap. 5)

It is clear enough from this passage, surely, that the convulsed era that Carlyle wrote about is not yet over. In *Sartor Resartus*, an early book, he suggests that we may be at present but half-way through it. Adapting from Jean-Paul (two of whose *novellen* Carlyle translated) a term chosen by the German as the title of a book of his never translated into English, he refers many times both in *Sartor* and in *The French Revolution* to the *Palingenesia* or 'Phoenix Death-Birth of Human Society', and hints that this is a process which may be expected to last *three hundred years* ! Louis-Claude de Saint-Martin referred to the French Revolution as 'an epitome of the Last Judgement', and if we take the French Revolution as the convulsive overture with which the whole Palingenesic era began, then we may still have a little less than a hundred and fifty years more of *Sturm und Drang* and indeed of all too realistically prophesied fire-consummation to look forward to before we 'find ourselves again in a Living Society, and no longer fighting but working'.

> For the rest, in what year of grace such Phoenix-cremation will be completed, we need not ask. The law of Perseverence is among the deepest in man : by nature he hates change ; seldom will he quit his old house till it has actually fallen about his ears.
>
> (*Sartor Resartus*)

This conception of the Palingenesic nature of the Present Age is one of the key ideas to his whole work. It was this that led him to be drawn for a short while to the teachings of Saint-Simon, to whom he refers in passing in *Sartor Resartus* ; though he followed the advice of Goethe, who wrote to him : 'From the St. Simonian Society pray hold yourself aloof.' In the same connexion, although there is no indication that Carlyle was acquainted with the writings of either of them, one might mention Ballanche and Fourier.

In his Inaugural Address on being installed as Rector of Edinburgh University, in 1866, Carlyle said : 'I need not hide from you, young Gentlemen, that you have got into a very troublous epoch of the world. . . .'

> Look where one will, revolution has come upon us. We have got into the age of revolutions. All kinds of things are

coming to be subjected to fire, as it were : hotter and hotter blows the element round everything. . . . It is evident that whatever is not inconsumable, made of *asbestos*, will have to be burnt, in this world. Nothing other will stand the heat it is getting exposed to.

It was in *Chartism* that Carlyle delivered his stirring clarion-call on the subject of Education. It is difficult to-day fully to realize how great was the need for such a call, as difficult perhaps as it is nowadays to realize what was then, before the turn of the nineteenth century, the position of women in society. The situation both of women and of education has been vastly altered ; but not so much so that we do not need to be reminded that they both still constitute a problem for the social conscience. Carlyle's words have lost none of their force, and may well serve to indicate what Britain's true greatness as an empire has lain in recognizing in some degree :

> To impart the gift of thinking to those who cannot think, and yet who could in that case think : this, one would imagine, was the first function a government had to set about discharging. Were it not a cruel thing to see, in any province of an empire the inhabitants living all mutilated in their limbs, each strong man with his right arm lamed ? How much crueller to find the strong soul, with its eyes still sealed, its eyes extinct so that it sees not ! Light has come into the world, but to this poor peasant it has come in vain. For six thousand years the Sons of Adam, in sleepless effort, have been devising, doing, discovering ; in mysterious infinite indissoluble communion, warring, a little band of brothers, against the great black empire of Necessity and Night ; they have accomplished such a conquest and conquests : and to this man it is all as if it had not been. . . .
>
> Heavier wrong is not done under the sun. It lasts from year to year, from century to century ; the blinded sire slaves himself out, and leaves a blinded son ; and men, made in the image of God, continue as two-legged beasts of labour ;—and in the largest empire of the world, it is a debate whether a small fraction of the Revenue of one Day (£30,000 is but that) shall, after Thirteen Centuries, be laid out on it, or not laid out on it.

Have we Governors, have we Teachers; have we had a Church these thirteen hundred years? What is an Overseer of souls, an Archoverseer, Archiepiscopus? Is he something? If so, let him lay his hand on his heart, and say what thing!

(At this point, we might to-day just hear, through the mighty roar of world-wide ballyhoo, a distant voice affirming : ' I am Ezra Pound.')

Education is not only an eternal duty, but has at length become even a temporary and ephemeral one, which the necessities of the hour will oblige us to look after. These twenty-four million labouring men, if their affairs remain unregulated, chaotic, will burn ricks and mills; reduce us, themselves and the world into ashes and ruin. Simply their affairs cannot remain unregulated, chaotic; but must be regulated, brought into some kind of order. What intellect were able to regulate them? The intellect of a Bacon, the energy of a Luther, if left to their own strength, might pause in dismay before such a task; a Bacon and Luther added together, to be perpetual prime minister over us, could not do it. What can? Only twenty-four million ordinary intellects, once awakened into action; these, well presided over, may. Intellect, insight, is the discernment of order in disorder; it is the discovery of the will of Nature, of God's will; the beginning of the capability to walk according to that. With perfect intellect, were such possible without perfect morality, the world would be perfect; its efforts unerringly correct, its results continually successful, its condition faultless. Intellect is like light; the Chaos becomes a world under it : *fiat lux*. . . . According as there was intellect or no intellect in the individuals, will the general conclusion they make-out embody itself as a world-healing Truth and Wisdom, or as a baseless fateful Hallucination, a Chimæra breathing *not* fabulous fire !

Carlyle, the ardent, profoundly reverent and grateful pupil of Goethe, was one of his best translators and interpreters and became himself of all English writers of the nineteenth century indisputably the greatest Teacher. He believed that if he tried his utmost to communicate the truths he could most clearly see, that men, willingly or unwillingly, would listen to him, that they would recognize the truth insofar as he could succeed in communicating it to them, and that eventually they would be changed by it. His whole life was built on this faith; the gratitude of millions must have proved to him, had he lived till the end of the nineteenth century only, that it was not faith in an illusion. It was, in fact, faith in the essential *respectability*, in the stricter sense of the word, of the common man, insofar as the latter is still, in the strict sense of the word, an individual, which as a member of the crowd he is *not*.

Since Carlyle's challenge to the governors of England on the subject of Education in *Chartism* (1840), there have been ever increasing educational improvements of every description, ever vaster sums expended annually on the nation's education, or at least on the larger if not the best part of it, and yet the world still seems full of people whose education has not made them proud of it, and people whose education has made them proud of it for the wrong reasons; sufficiently full at any rate to make it seem that the masses are perhaps uneducable. But the majority of 'educated people' may be depended on to agree in principle that unless one has a proper respect for education and a sense of the true equality that it alone can bring, one can hardly be expected to be other than a pseudo-democrat.

The idea of literature being educational in intention seems to-day almost uncouth; but it has not always been so regarded. That literature requires a higher degree of education in the reader than the average man can at present be presumed to possess is quite a common assumption; and the display of considerable erudition is by some students thought not to be an incidental accompaniment of literary ability but invariably an indication of merit.

Carlyle's conception of literature is one that much needs reconsidering in these days. It is outlined succinctly enough in the following passages:

> Literature is but a branch of Religion, and always participates in its character: however, in our time, it is the only branch that

still shows any greenness ; and, as some think, must one day become the main stem.

(*Characteristics*)

Genius, Poet : do we know what these words mean ? An inspired Soul once more vouchsafed us, direct from Nature's own great fire-heart, to see the Truth, and speak it, and do it ; Nature's own sacred voice heard once more athwart the dreary boundless element of hearsaying and canting, of twaddle and poltroonery, in which the bewildered Earth, nigh perishing, has *lost its way*. Hear once more, ye bewildered mortals ; listen once again to a voice from the inner Light-sea and Flame-sea, Nature's and Truth's own heart ; know the Fact of your Existence what it is, put away the Cant of it which it is *not* ; and knowing, do, and let it be well with you !

(*Past and Present*, Bk. II, Chap. 9)

'Beyond all ages, our Age admonishes whatsoever thinking or writing man it has : Oh speak to me, some wise intelligible speech ; your wise meaning, in the shortest and clearest way ; behold I am dying for want of wise meaning, and insight into the devouring fact : speak, if you have any wisdom ! As to song so-called, and your fiddling talent,—even if you have one, much more if you have none,—we will talk of that a couple of centuries hence, when things are calmer again. Homer shall be thrice welcome ; but only when Troy is *taken* : alas, while the siege lasts, and battle's fury rages everywhere, what can I do with the Homer ? I want Achilles and Odysseus, and am enraged to see them trying to be Homers !'

(*Life of Sterling*, Part III, Chap. 1)

Literature, when noble, is not easy ; but only when ignoble. Literature too is a quarrel, and internecine duel, with the whole World of Darkness that lies without one and within one ;— rather a hard fight at times, even with the three pound ten secure. Thou, where thou art, wrestle and duel along, cheerfully to the end ; and make no remarks.

(*Past and Present*, Bk. II, Chap. 12)

But I say, have you computed what a distance forwards it may be towards some *new* Psalm of David done with our new appliances, and much improved wind-instruments, grammatical and other? This is the distance of the new Golden Age, my friend; not less than that, I lament to say! And the centuries that intervene are a foul, agonistic welter through the Stygian seas of mud: a long *Scavenger Age*, inevitable where the Mother of Abominations has long dwelt.

(*Latter-Day Pamphlet*, No. VIII, 'Jesuitism', August 1850)

Of Literature, in all ways, be shy rather than otherwise, at present! There where thou art, work, work; whatsoever thy hand findeth to do, do it,—with the hand of a man, not of a phantasm; be that thy unnoticed blessedness and exceeding great reward. Thy words, let them be few, and well ordered. Love silence rather than speech in these tragic days, when for very speaking, the voice of man has fallen inarticulate to man; and hearts, in this loud babbling, sit dark and dumb towards one another. Witty,—above all, O be not witty: none of us is bound to be witty, under penalties; to be wise and true we all are, under the terriblest penalties!

(*Latter-Day Pamphlet*, No. V, 'Stump-Orator', May 1850)

And yet our Heroic Men of Letters do teach, govern, are kings, priests, or what you like to call them; intrinsically there is no preventing it by any means whatever. The world *has* to obey him who thinks and sees in the world. The world can alter the manner of that; can either have it as blessed continuous summer sunshine, or as unblessed black thunder and tornado,—with unspeakable difference of profit for the world! The manner of it is very alterable; the matter and fact of it is not alterable by any power under the sky. Light; or, failing that, lightning: the world can take its choice. Not whether we call an Odin god, prophet, priest, or what we call him; but whether we believe the word he tells us: there it all lies. If it be a true word, we shall have to believe it; believing it, we shall have to do it. What *name* or welcome we give him or it, is a point that concerns ourselves mainly. *It*, the new Truth, new deeper revealing of the Secret of this Universe, is verily of the nature of a message from on high; and must and will have itself obeyed.

(*On Heroes and Hero-Worship*, Lecture V)

The convulsive era of which Carlyle wrote, as I said just now, is the same as that in which we are still living. These words, though written in 1831, have an astonishingly topical present relevance :

> The doom of the Old has long been pronounced, and irrevocable ; the Old has passed away : but, alas, the New appears not in its stead ; the Time is still in pangs of travail with the New. Man has walked by the light of conflagrations, and amid the sound of falling cities ; and now there is darkness, and long watching till it be morning. The voice even of the faithful can but exclaim : ' As yet struggles the twelfth hour of the Night : birds of darkness are on the wing, spectres uproar, the dead walk, the living dream. Thou, Eternal Providence, wilt cause the day to dawn ! '
>
> Such being the condition, temporal and spiritual, of the world at our Epoch, can we wonder that the world ' listens to itself ', and struggles and writhes, everywhere externally and internally, like a thing in pain ? Nay, is not even this unhealthy action of the world's Organization, if the symptom of universal disease, yet also the symptom and sole means of restoration and cure ? . . . Innumerable ' Philosophies of Man ', contending in boundless hubbub, must annihilate each other, before an inspired Poesy and Faith for Man can fashion itself together.
>
> <div style="text-align:right">(<i>Characteristics</i>)</div>

The message of Carlyle for the present generation is also particularly that which he articulated in his book on his friend John Sterling, a man who failed to become either an important poet or a religious reformer, but spent his life struggling to give expression to his desire for a wider recognition of true greatness and nobility, and was perhaps a figure representative of the purest idealism[1] of his generation.

> Old hidebound Toryism, being now openly cracking towards some incurable disruption . . . long recognized by all the world, and now at last obliged to recognize its very self, for an overgrown Imposture, supporting itself not by human reason, but by flunkey blustering and brazen lying, superadded to mere

[1] *Idealism* : in the loose and unphilosophical sense of the word, referring to ideal *aim*, not pure *idea*.

brute force, could be no creed for young Sterling and his friends. In all things he and they were liberals, and, as was natural at this stage, democrats ; contemplating root-and-branch innovation by aid of the hustings and ballotbox. Hustings and ballotbox had speedily to vanish out of Sterling's thoughts ; but the character of root-and-branch innovator, essentially of 'Radical Reformer' was indelible with him, and under all forms could be traced as his character through life.

... Piety of heart, a certain reality of religious faith, was always Sterling's, the gift of nature to him which he would not and could not throw away ; but I find at this time his religion is as good as altogether Ethnic, Greekish, what Goethe calls the Heathen form of religion. The Church, with her articles, is without relation to him. And along with obsolete spiritualisms, he sees all manner of obsolete thrones and big-wigged temporalities ; and for them also can prophesy, and wish, only a speedy doom. Doom inevitable, registered in Heaven's Chancery from the beginning of days, doom unalterable as the pillars of the world ; the gods are angry, and all nature groans, till this doom of eternal justice be fulfilled.

... We shall have to admit, nay it will behove us to see and practically know, for ourselves and him and others, that the essence of this creed, in times like ours, was right and not wrong. That, however the ground and form of it might change, essentially it was the monition of his natal genius to this as it is to every brave man ; the behest of all his clear insight into this Universe, the message of Heaven through him, which he could not suppress, but was inspired and compelled to utter in this world by such methods as he had. There for him lay the first commandment ; *this* is what it would have been the unforgivable sin to swerve from and desert ; the treason of treasons for him, it were there ; compared with which all other sins are venial !

(*Life of Sterling*, Chap. 7)

At first sight, I think it would not seem that this biography of a gifted young man who accomplished nothing, though he never ceased to be a seeker, were among the books of Carlyle's most likely to have interest for the modern reader. But it does contain the expression of an attitude towards established Religion which still, if anything even more than when it was written, is the attitude of a mature and *free* religious mind (and a religious mind that is not free is merely a superstitious mind).

> This battle, universal in our sad epoch, of 'all old things passing away' against 'all things becoming new', has its summary and animating heart in that of Radicalism against Church : there, as in its flaming core, and point of focal splendour, does the heroic worth that lies in each side of the quarrel most clearly disclose itself; and Sterling was the man, above many, to recognize such worth on both sides. Natural enough, in such a one, that the light of Radicalism having gone out in darkness for him, the opposite splendour should next rise as the chief, and invite his loyalty till it also failed. In one form or the other, such an aberration was not unlikely for him. But an aberration, especially in this form, we may certainly call it. No man of Sterling's veracity, had he clearly consulted his own heart, or had his own heart been capable of clearly responding, and not been dazzled and bewildered by transient fantasies and theosophic moonshine, could have undertaken this function [*i.e. that of the priesthood*]. His heart would have answered : 'No, thou canst not. What is incredible to thee, thou shalt not, at thy soul's peril, attempt to believe ! . . . Elsewhither for a refuge, or die here. Go to Perdition if thou must,—but not with a lie in thy mouth ; by the Eternal Maker, no !'

Commenting on a letter from France to himself from his friend Sterling, Carlyle writes as follows, giving a forceful indication of his attitude in maturity, towards all outward forms of religion in the modern world :

> Tholuck, Schleiermacher, and the war of articles and rubrics were left in the far distance ; Nature's blue skies, and awful eternal verities, were once more around one, and small still voices, admonitory of many things, could in the beautiful solitude freely reach the heart. Theologies, rubrics, surplices, church articles, and this enormous ever-repeated thrashing of the straw ? A world of rotten straw ; thrashed all into powder ; filling the Universe and blotting out the stars and worlds : —Heaven pity you with such a thrashing floor for world, and its draggled dirty farthing-candle for sun ! There is surely

other worship possible for the heart of man; there should be other work, or none at all, for the intellect and creative faculty of man!

On another letter to him, from Rome, Carlyle makes even more scornful comment:

> It is surely fit to recognize with admiring joy any glimpse of the Beautiful and the Eternal that is hung out for us, in colour, in form or tone, in canvas, stone, or atmospheric air, and made accessible by any sense, in this world: but it is greatly fitter still (little as we are used that way) to shudder in pity and abhorrence over the scandalous tragedy, transcendent nadir of human ugliness and contemptibility, which under the daring title of religious worship, and practical recognition of the Highest God, daily and hourly everywhere transacts itself there. And, alas, not there only, but elsewhere, everywhere more or less; whereby our sense is so blunted to it;—whence, in all provinces of human life, these tears!

If these words are vehement, they are not more so than those which Carlyle had 'quoted' from a pseudonymous *alter ego* of his, whom he calls *Crabbe*, in the Seventh of the *Latter-Day Pamphlets* ('Hudson's Statue', 1 July 1850), on the subject of the 'so-called Christian *Clerus*' (he himself calls it 'a wild passage'):

> Legions of them, in their black or other gowns, I still meet in every country; masquerading, in strange costume of body, and still stranger of soul; mumming, primming, grimacing,—poor devils, shamming, and endeavouring not to sham: this is the sad fact. Brave men many of them, after their sort; and in a position which we may admit to be wonderful and dreadful! On the outside of their heads some singular headgear, tulip-mitre, felt coal-scuttle, purple hat; and in the inside,—I must say, such a Theory of God Almighty's Universe as I, for my part, am right thankful to have no concern with at all! I think, on the whole, as broken-winged, self-strangled, monstrous a mass of incoherent incredibilities, as ever dwelt in the human brain before. O God, giver of Light, hater of Darkness, of Hypocrisy and Cowardice, how long, how long!

These are not the words of an anti-religious man, but of a religious man of unusual earnestness ; and they show that it is not altogether a vagary to associate Carlyle's name with that of Nietzsche : here, far more than in any supposed affinity of the Carlylian Hero with the Superman, may be perceived the real ground of any such connexion as there may be.

That Carlyle's attitude towards the rest of his fellow men had in it a certain amount of arrogance, his remark about Democracy : 'Twenty-seven millions, mostly fools', is sufficient indication ; but it also contained such genuine humility and so clear a realization of the insignificance of the greatest man in relation to the inscrutable All, that he was ever incapable of the passionate self-assertiveness and dionysian *hubris* that carried Nietzsche off into his final madness. His religious radicalism is more adult and sane than that of the Prophet of Superman, while being healthier and less strained than the agonizingly scruple-tormented Kierkegaard's.

> The essence of all ' religion ' that was and that ever will be is to make men *free*. Who is he that, in this life-pilgrimage, will consecrate himself at all hazards to obey God and God's servants, and to disobey the Devil and his ? With pious valour this free man walks through the roaring tumults, invincibly the way whither he is bound. To him in the waste Saharas, through the grim solitudes peopled by galvanized corpses and doleful creatures, there is a lode-star ; and his path, whatever those of others be, is towards the Eternal. A man well worth consulting, and taking note of, about matters temporal.

To-day once more it is important to recognize in what Carlyle expresses in the passages quoted above the most essential part of his message as a religious man and a prophet. If anyone not really familiar with Carlyle's writings should be puzzled by remembering, in this connexion, the often repeated expression ' Hebrew old-clothes ', which recurs constantly throughout his works, he may be enlightened by these words from Martin Buber's outstanding work of exegesis of the Hebrew Prophets of the Old Testament: 'The leader-God ... wants to root out of men's hearts the notion that it is possible to satisfy Him merely with worship and cult.'[1] And the word worship in this sentence is not to be confused, be it noted, with the meaning that Carlyle most often gives it; for Carlyle, worship was first and last the immediate reaction of *sincerity*, and without sincerity, nothing, nothing, nothing, that man, be he never so pious and never so highly consecrated and ordained, can either say or do, will ever be satisfying to God. But his own words can best tell us what Carlyle understood by the word Worship:

> I will insert this also, in a lower strain, from Sauerteig's *Aesthetische Springwurzeln*. 'Worship?' says he: 'Before that inane tumult of Hearsay filled men's heads, while the world yet lay silent, and the heart true and open, many things were Worship! To the primeval man whatsoever good came, descended on him (as, in mere fact, it ever does) direct from God; whatsoever duty lay visible for him, this a Supreme God had prescribed. To the present hour I ask thee, Who else? For the primeval man, in whom dwelt Thought, this Universe was all a Temple; Life everywhere a Worship.'
>
> (*Past and Present*, Bk. III, Chap. 15)

The position of Carlyle in importance I would reckon to be somewhere about mid-way between two very great and extremely different men of the nineteenth century, Søren Kierkegaard on the one hand, and Walt Whitman on the other. All three alike are particularly to be distinguished as having at the basis of their work what Carlyle called 'an open loving heart'.

Both Carlyle and Kierkegaard were poets who wrote in prose. Both were anti-romantic romantics and anti-idealist Post-Hegelians. Both might well be called 'knights of faith'; both thought of themselves as 'witnesses to the truth', and suffered hostility and derision in consequence.

---

[1] Martin Buber: "The Prophetic Tradition." Eng. trans. 1950.

Both were virtuosos of homiletic eloquence, who fully realized the vanity of all eloquence that fails to move the hearer's heart. Above all, it is in the way they both understood the fatal significance in the modern age of the disintegration of 'society' into 'coteries', 'swarmeries' and 'crowds', that the closeness of Carlyle's thought to Kierkegaard's should be seen. Every analysis of the modern crisis of civilization that fails to take account of Kierkegaard's and Carlyle's criticisms of the Crowd and of the anti-Christian spirit which invariably animates it (for it is always the Crowd that cries 'Give us Barabbas!'), is bound to lead to further misunderstanding of all present social problems.

In situating Carlyle between Kierkegaard and Whitman, I was thinking also of the pessimism and the optimism of Carlyle; on the one hand 'this British Hamlet from Cheyne Row, more puzzling than the Danish one' (as Whitman described him), and on the other the enthusiast whose vision of 'the divine idea of the world' and faith in the necessity of fire for the new-birth of the Phoenix enabled him to see 'before us ... the boundless Time, with its as yet uncreated and unconquered Continents and Eldorados, which we, even we, have to conquer, to create....'

It might well be considered that it is just this middle situation of Carlyle that makes him a writer with a message of special value to the present generation, if it could but be clearly disengaged from the misconceptions and misinterpretations that have long accumulated about his work, and which are partly the result of a sort of self-protective instinct in the many who do not wish to be confronted by the real significance of what the prophet has to tell them, and from those parts of Carlyle's writings which really are not of such immediate relevance to us now (and these would probably in all amount only to the lesser part of his work). By 'middle situation', I mean that in which it is possible to see that there is no genuine hope, except that which can survive a long and courageously searching look at the worst; only from this position, it would seem, can one see the worst, and still be able to see enough of the purposes of the Eternal to be able to live without wasting our potentialities.

Carlyle cannot be claimed either by the Left or by the Right. He was too faithful to his vision of 'the Divine Idea of the World' to be a partisan of any hard-and-fast ideology; more than heroism, he worshipped the Objective. This briefest of introductions to his writings has not attempted to give any idea of *The French Revolution* or to do justice to Carlyle's conception of History and the art of the Historian. Social and Literary Historians in general cannot yet be said to have done this fully either.

THOMAS CARLYLE
A
Select Bibliography

(Place of publication London, unless stated otherwise.)

Bibliographies:

A CATALOGUE OF THE DR. SAMUEL A. JONES CARLYLE COLLECTION. Compiled by M. E. Wead. Ann Arbor, Mich. (1919).

A BIBLIOGRAPHY OF THOMAS CARLYLE'S WRITINGS AND ANA. By I. W. Dyer. Portland, Maine (1928).

Collected Editions:

COLLECTED WORKS, 16 vols. (1857–8).

LIBRARY EDITION, 34 vols. (1868–71).

THE ASHBURTON EDITION, 20 vols. Chapman and Hall (1885–8).

CENTENARY EDITION, 30 vols. Chapman and Hall (1896–9).
The most complete edition.

Separate Works:

[ELEMENTS OF GEOMETRY AND TRIGONOMETRY. Translated from the French of A. M. Legendre.] Edinburgh (1824). *Translation.*
The translation and the Introduction (' On Proportion ') are by Carlyle.

[WILHELM MEISTER'S APPRENTICESHIP. A Novel from the German of Goethe.] 3 vols. Edinburgh (1824). *Translation.*
Translated by Carlyle: New edition, revised, including ' Wilhelm Meister's Travels ', 1839.

THE LIFE OF FRIEDRICH SCHILLER. Comprehending an Examination of his Works (1825). *Biography.*
Originally published in the *London Magazine* 1823–4. The German translation (1830) is by Goethe.

[GERMAN ROMANCE. Specimens of its Chief Authors with Biographical and Critical Notices.] 4 vols. Edinburgh (1827). *Translation.*
Translated by Carlyle. Contains extracts from Musaeus, Fouqué, Tieck, Hoffman, Richter, and Goethe.

SARTOR RESARTUS : the Life and Opinions of Herr Teufelsdröckh. In three Books. With a Preface by R. W. Emerson, Boston (1836), London (1838). *Essays.*
Originally published in *Fraser's Magazine* 1833-4. Definitive edition by A. MachMechan, Boston, 1896.

THE FRENCH REVOLUTION. A History. 3 vols. (1837). *History.*
Authoritative editions by C. R. L. Fletcher, 1902 ; J. H. Rose, 1902 ; C. F. Harrold, New York, 1937.

CRITICAL AND MISCELLANEOUS ESSAYS. Collected and Republished (from periodicals, etc.). 4 vols. Boston (1838 ; London 1839). *Essays.* Including 'Characteristics'.
Additional essays were included in subsequent editions, the fullest being in five volumes, 1899.

CHARTISM (1840). *Essay.*

ON HEROES, HERO-WORSHIP, AND THE HEROIC IN HISTORY. Six lectures. Reported with Emendations and Additions (1841). *Lectures.*
Definitive edition by A. MachMechan, Boston, 1901.

PAST AND PRESENT (1843). *Essays.*
Edited by A. M. D. Hughes, Oxford, 1921, and by E. Rhys (Everyman's Library).

LETTERS AND SPEECHES OF OLIVER CROMWELL : WITH ELUCIDATIONS. 2 vols. (1845 ; enlarged edition in 3 vols., 1846). *History.*
Edited by W. A. Shaw (Everyman's Library).

LATTER-DAY PAMPHLETS (1850). *Satirical Essays.*
Contains : 'The Present Time' ; 'Model Prisons' ; 'Downing Street' ; 'The New Downing Street' ; 'Stump Orator' ; 'Parliaments' ; 'Hudson's Statue' ; 'Jesuitism'.

THE LIFE OF JOHN STERLING (1851). *Biography.*
World's Classics edition, ed. W. H. White, 1907.

THE HISTORY OF FRIEDRICH II OF PRUSSIA, CALLED FREDERICK THE GREAT. 6 vols. (1858-65). *History.*
Published in an abridged form, ed. A. M. D. Hughes, Oxford, 1916.

ON THE CHOICE OF BOOKS. With a Memoir by J. C. Hotten (1866). *Lecture.*
Originally delivered as an inaugural address on being installed as Rector of the University of Edinburgh, 2 April 1866.

SELECT BIBLIOGRAPHY

THE EARLY KINGS OF NORWAY : also AN ESSAY ON THE PORTRAITS OF JOHN KNOX (1875). *Essays.*
Reprinted from *Fraser's Magazine*, 1875.

REMINISCENCES. Edited by J. A. Froude. 2 vols. (1881). *Autobiography.*
Everyman's Library edition, 1932.

REMINISCENCES OF MY IRISH JOURNEY IN 1849. With a Preface by J. A. Froude (1882). *Autobiography.*

LAST WORDS OF THOMAS CARLYLE ON TRADES-UNIONS, PROMOTERISM, THE SIGNS OF THE TIMES. With a Preface by J. C. Aitken. Edinburgh (1882). *Essays.*

LETTERS AND MEMORIALS OF JANE WELSH CARLYLE. Prepared for publication by Thomas Carlyle. Edited by J. A. Froude. 3 vols. (1883).

LAST WORDS OF THOMAS CARLYLE. Wotton Reinfred : A Romance. Edited by R. Preuss (1892). Excursion (futile enough) to Paris. Letters to Varnhagen von Ense. *Essays.*

HISTORICAL SKETCHES OF NOTABLE PERSONS AND EVENTS IN THE REIGNS OF JAMES I AND CHARLES I. Ed. by A. Carlyle (1898).

TWO NOTE-BOOKS OF THOMAS CARLYLE, from 23 March 1822—16 May 1832. Edited by C. E. Norton. New York (1898). Printed for members of the Grolier Club.

NEW LETTERS AND MEMORIALS OF JANE WELSH CARLYLE. Annotated by Thomas Carlyle. Edited by A. Carlyle and Sir J. Crichton-Browne. 2 vols. (1903).
Note.—Apart from the reprints of separate works in Everyman's Library and the World's Classics (see above), there are selections of Carlyle's writings in *The Carlyle Anthology*, New York (1876) ; *The Pocket Carlyle* (1908) ; *Selected Essays* (1909) ; *The Best of Carlyle* (1923).

LETTERS ADDRESSED TO MRS. BASIL MONTAGUE AND B. W. PROCTER. Edited by A. B. Procter (1881).
Reprinted with a Preface by Sir E. Gosse. Lakeland, Mich. (1907).

THE CORRESPONDENCE OF CARLYLE AND EMERSON, 1834-1872. Edited by C. E. Norton. 2 vols. (1883).

EARLY LETTERS. Edited by C. E. Norton. 2 vols. (1886). ((i) 1814-21 ; (ii) 1821-6). See also LETTERS (1826-36). 2 vols. (1888) by the same editor.

CORRESPONDENCE BETWEEN GOETHE AND CARLYLE. Edited by C. E. Norton (1887).

EARLY LETTERS OF JANE WELSH CARLYLE. Edited by D. G. Ritchie (1899).
Contains a few later letters as well as some by Thomas Carlyle, her husband.

LETTERS TO HIS YOUNGEST SISTER. Edited with an Introductory Essay, by C. T. Copeland. Boston (1899).

NEW LETTERS. Edited and Annotated by A. Carlyle. 2 vols. (1904).

THE LOVE LETTERS OF CARLYLE AND JANE WELSH. Edited by A. Carlyle. 2 vols. (1909).

LETTERS TO JOHN STUART MILL, JOHN STERLING, AND ROBERT BROWNING. Edited by A. Carlyle (1923).

JANE WELSH CARLYLE : LETTERS TO HER FAMILY (1839-63). Edited by L. Huxley (1924).

NEW LETTERS. Edited by W. A. Speck. Yale Review, New Haven (1926).
Letters to Eckermann.

LETTERS OF THOMAS CARLYLE TO WILLIAM GRAHAM. Edited by J. Graham, Jnr. Oxford (1950).

Some Critical and Biographical Studies :

L'IDEALISME ANGLAIS. Etude sur Carlyle, par H. A. Taine. Paris (1864).

THOMAS CARLYLE : THE MAN AND THE TEACHER, by D. Hodge. Edinburgh (1873).

MEMOIRS OF THE LIFE AND WRITINGS OF THOMAS CARLYLE, with Personal Reminiscences and Selections from his Private Letters, by H. Shepherd and C. N. Williamson. 2 vols. (1881).

THOMAS CARLYLE : THE MAN AND HIS BOOKS, by W. H. Wylie (1881).

THE PHILOSOPHY OF CARLYLE, by E. D. Mead. Boston (1881).

THOMAS CARLYLE, by H. J. Nicoll. Edinburgh (1881).

THOMAS CARLYLE, by M. D. Conway (1881).

SELECT BIBLIOGRAPHY

NATIONAL LESSONS FROM THE LIFE AND WORKS OF THOMAS CARLYLE, by A. Francison (1881).

THOMAS CARLYLE. A History of the First Forty Years of his Life, 1795–1835, by J. A. Froude. 2 vols. (1882).
See also the same author's controversial *Thomas Carlyle : a History of his Life in London*, 1834–81. 2 vols. 1884, and *My Relations with Carlyle*, 1903.

CARLYLE PERSONALLY AND IN HIS WRITINGS (TWO LECTURES), by D. Masson (1885).

CARLYLE AND THE OPEN SECRET OF HIS LIFE, by H. Larkin (1886).

SOME PERSONAL REMINISCENCES OF CARLYLE, by A. J. Symington. Paisley (1886).

GOETHE AND CARLYLE : An Inaugural Address delivered to the Goethe Society, 28 May 1886, by F. M. Müller (1886).

THE LIFE OF THOMAS CARLYLE, by R. Garnett (1887).
Contains a Bibliography by J. P. Anderson.

THE STORY OF THOMAS CARLYLE, by A. S. Arnold (1888).

THOMAS CARLYLE, by J. Nichol (1892).
In the English Men of Letters series.

CONVERSATIONS WITH CARLYLE, by Sir C. G. Duffy (1892).

CARLYLE'S PLACE IN LITERATURE, by F. Harrison (1894).

THE CARLYLES' CHELSEA HOME, by R. Blunt (1895).
The house in Cheyne Row, now the property of the National Trust, is open to the public and contains books, manuscripts, relics, etc., and much of the original furnishings.

THOMAS CARLYLE, by H. C. MacPherson. Edinburgh (1896).

MR. FROUDE AND CARLYLE, by D. A. Wilson (1898).
See the same author's *The Truth about Carlyle*, 1913.

THOMAS CARLYLE : Essai biographique et critique. Par E. Barthélemy. Paris (1900).

CARLYLE : A Brief Account of his Life and Writings, by B. W. Matz (1902).

THE CARLYLE COUNTRY : With a Study of Carlyle's Life, by J. M. Sloan (1904).

THE MAKING OF CARLYLE, an Experiment in Biographical Explication, by R. S. Craig (1908).

CARLYLE'S FIRST LOVE : Margaret Gordon, Lady Bannerman, by R. C. Archibald (1909).

THOMAS CARLYLE : A Study of his Literary Apprenticeship, 1814–31, by W. S. Johnson. New Haven (1911).

CARLYLE, par Louis Cazamian. Paris (1913).
English translation by E. K. Brown. New York (1932).

A GUIDE TO CARLYLE, by Augustus Ralli. 2 vols. (1920).

THE LIFE OF THOMAS CARLYLE, by D. A. Wilson. 6 vols. (1923–34).
Vol. i 'Carlyle till Marriage, 1795–1826' (1923).
    ii 'Carlyle till *The French Revolution*, 1826–1837' (1924).
    iii 'Carlyle on Cromwell and Others, 1837–1847' (1925).
    iv 'Carlyle at His Zenith, 1848–1853' (1927).
    v 'Carlyle to Threescore-and-ten, 1853–1865' (1929).
    vi 'Carlyle in Old Age, 1865–1881' (1934), completed by D. W. MacArthur.

CARLYLE AND MILL : MYSTIC AND UTILITARIAN, by E. E. Neff. New York (1924).
See the same author's CARLYLE, 1932.

THOMAS CARLYLE, by M. A. Hamilton (1926).

CARLYLE : His Rise and Fall, by N. Young (1927).

THE PRINCIPAL PORTRAITS AND STATUES OF THOMAS CARLYLE, by A. S. Barrett (1928).

JANE WELSH AND JANE CARLYLE, by E. Drew (1928).

CARLYLE : SA PREMIÈRE FORTUNE LITTERAIRE EN FRANCE, 1825–1865, par A. C. Taylor. Paris (1929).
See the same author's CARLYLE ET LA PENSEÉ LATINE, Paris, 1937.

THE TWO CARLYLES, by O. H. Burdett (1930).

FROUDE AND CARLYLE, by W. H. Dunn (1930).

CARLYLE AND HITLER, by H. J. C. Grierson. Cambridge (1933).
The Adamson Lecture in Manchester University.

CARLYLE AND GERMAN THOUGHT, 1819–1834, by C. F. Harrold. New Haven (1934).

CARLYLE, by D. Lammond (1934).

SELECT BIBLIOGRAPHY

CARLYLE, L'HOMME ET L'OEUVRE, par V. G. Basch. Paris (1938).

CARLYLE : PROPHET OF TODAY, by F. A. Lea (1943).

A CENTURY OF HERO-WORSHIP. A Study of the Idea of Heroism, in Carlyle and Nietzsche, by E. R. Bentley. New York (1944). See the same author's *The Cult of the Superman*, 1949.

JANE WELSH CARLYLE : A New Selection of her Letters, edited by T. Bliss (1950).

NECESSARY EVIL : A LIFE OF JANE WELSH CARLYLE, by L. E. E. Hanson (1951).

THOMAS CARLYLE : THE LIFE AND TIMES OF A PROPHET, by J. Symons (1951).

INDEX OF ESSAYS AND PAPERS

(*The title in brackets refers to the main title of the book*)

Abbot Hugo (*Past and Present*)
Abbot Samson (*Past and Present*)
Abbot's Troubles, The (*Past and Present*)
Abbot's Ways, The (*Past and Present*)
Aristocracies (*Past and Present*)
Aristocracy of Talent (*Past and Present*)
Aslauga's Knight (trans.) (*Centenary Edition*)
Baillie the Covenanter (*Critical and Miscellaneous Essays*)
Beginnings, The (*Past and Present*)
Biography (*Critical and Miscellaneous Essays*)
Boswell's Life of Johnson (*Critical and Miscellaneous Essays*)
Bribery Committee (*Past and Present*)
Burns (*Critical and Miscellaneous Essays*)
Cagliostro, Count (*Critical and Miscellaneous Essays*)
Canvassing, The (*Past and Present*)
Captains of Industry (*Past and Present*)
Characteristics (*Critical and Miscellaneous Essays*)
Chartism (*Critical and Miscellaneous Essays*)
Consummation of Scepticism (*Centenary Edition*)
Corn-Law Rhymes (*Critical and Miscellaneous Essays*)
Cruthers and Jonson (*Memoirs of Carlyle; Critical and Miscellaneous Essays*)
Dante—the Italians (*Centenary Edition*)
Death of Charles Buller (*Memoirs of Carlyle*)
Death of Edward Irvine, The (*Critical and Miscellaneous Essays*)
Death of Goethe, The (*Critical and Miscellaneous Essays*)
Democracy (*Past and Present*)
Diamond Necklace, The (*Critical and Miscellaneous Essays*)
Didactic, The (*Past and Present*)
Diderot (*Critical and Miscellaneous Essays*)
Downing Street (*Latter-Day Pamphlets*)
Early Kings of Norway (*Critical and Miscellaneous Essays*)
Eighteenth Century in England, The (*Centenary Edition*)
Election, The (*Past and Present*)
Election to the Long Parliament, An (*Critical and Miscellaneous Essays*)
English, The (*Past and Present*)

English, The (*Centenary Edition*)
Excursion (futile enough) to Paris (*Last Words*, 1892)
Faust's Curse (*Centenary Edition*)
Faustus (*Centenary Edition*)
Foque (*Critical and Miscellaneous Essays*)
Fractions (*Critical and Miscellaneous Essays*)
Francia, Dr. (*Critical and Miscellaneous Essays*)
German Literature of the Fourteenth and Fifteenth Centuries (*Critical and Miscellaneous Essays*)
German Playwrights (*Critical and Miscellaneous Essays*)
Germans, The (*Centenary Edition*)
Gifted, The (*Past and Present*)
Goethe (*Critical and Miscellaneous Essays*)
Goethe's 'Helena' (*Critical and Miscellaneous Essays*)
Goethe's Portrait (*Critical and Miscellaneous Essays*)
Goethe's Works (*Critical and Miscellaneous Essays*)
Golden Pot, The (trans.) (*Centenary Edition*)
Gospel of Dilettantism (*Past and Present*)
Gospel of Mammonism (*Past and Present*)
Government (*Past and Present*)
Happy (*Past and Present*)
Heintze's German Translation of Burns (*Centenary Edition*)
Henry of Essex (*Past and Present*)
Hero as Divinity, The (*On Heroes*)
Hero as King, The (*On Heroes*)
Hero as Man of Letters, The (*On Heroes*)
Hero as Poet, The (*On Heroes*)
Hero as Priest, The (*On Heroes*)
Hero as Prophet, The (*On Heroes*)
Hero-Worship (*Past and Present*)
Heyne, Life of (*Critical and Miscellaneous Essays*)
Hoffman (*Critical and Miscellaneous Essays*)
Homer : The Heroic Ages (*Centenary Edition*)
Hudson's Statue (*Latter-Day Pamphlets*)
In Parliament (*Past and Present*)
Inaugural Address at Edinburgh (*Critical and Miscellaneous Essays*)
Indian Meal (*Centenary Edition*)

Ireland and the British Chief Governor (*Memoirs of Carlyle*)
Irish Regiments of the New Era (*Memoirs of Carlyle*)
Jesuitism (*Latter-Day Pamphlets*)
Jocelin de Brakelond (*Past and Present*)
Labour (*Past and Present*)
Landed, The (*Past and Present*)
Landlord Edmund (*Past and Present*)
Latter Stages of the French-German War, 1870–1 (*Critical and Miscellaneous Essays*)
Legislation for Ireland (*Memoirs of Carlyle*)
Letter to the Editor of the London *Times* concerning Miss Lowe, A (*Centenary Edition*)
Luther's Psalm (*Critical and Miscellaneous Essays*)
Manchester Insurrection (*Past and Present*)
Metrical Legends of Exalted Characters (*Centenary Edition*)
Midas (*Past and Present*)
Middle Ages—Christianity (*Centenary Edition*)
Mirabeau (*Critical and Miscellaneous Essays*)
Model Prisons (*Latter-Day Pamphlets*)
Monk Samson (*Past and Present*)
Montaigne (*Critical and Miscellaneous Essays*)
Montesquieu (*Critical and Miscellaneous Essays*)
Montfaucon (*Centenary Edition*)
Montuela (*Centenary Edition*)
Moore, Dr. John (*Centenary Edition*)
Morrison Again (*Past and Present*)
Morrison's Pill (*Past and Present*)
Musaeus (*Critical and Miscellaneous Essays*)
National Exhibition of Scottish Portraits, The (*Critical and Miscellaneous Essays*)
Necker (*Critical and Miscellaneous Essays*)
Nelson (*Centenary Edition*)
Netherlands, The (*Montaigne; Critical and Miscellaneous Essays*)
New Downing Street, The (*Latter-Day Pamphlets*)
Newfoundland (*Centenary Edition*)
Nibelungen Lied, The (*Critical and Miscellaneous Essays*)
Nigger Question, The (*Critical and Miscellaneous Essays*)

INDEX OF ESSAYS AND PAPERS 43

Nimmo, Peter (*Memoirs of Carlyle*)
Norfolk (*Centenary Edition*)
Northamptonshire (*Montaigne*)
Novalis (*Critical and Miscellaneous Essays*)
Northumberland (*Centenary Edition*)
Novelle (*Critical and Miscellaneous Essays*)
Of Literature in General (*Centenary Edition*)
Of Modern German Literature (*Centenary Edition*)
On History (*Critical and Miscellaneous Essays*)
On History Again (*Critical and Miscellaneous Essays*)
On Trades-Unions (*Last Words*, 1882)
One Institution, The (*Past and Present*)
Opera, The (*Critical and Miscellaneous Essays*)
Over Production (*Past and Present*)
Park, Mungo (*Centenary Edition*)
Parliamentary History of The French Revolution, The (*Critical and Miscellaneous Essays*)
Parliaments (*Latter-Day Pamphlets*)
Permanence (*Past and Present*)
Petition on the Copyright Bill (*Critical and Miscellaneous Essays*)
Phenomena (*Past and Present*)
Philippe, Louis (*Memoirs of Carlyle*)
Pitt, Earl of Chatham, William (*Critical and Miscellaneous Essays*)
Pitt, The Younger, William (*Critical and Miscellaneous Essays*)
Plugson of Undershot (*Past and Present*)
Poems (*Critical and Miscellaneous Essays*)
Portrait of John Knox, The (*Critical and Miscellaneous Essays*)
Practical-Devotional (*Past and Present*)
Prefaces to the first and second editions of 'Wilhelm Meister' (*Critical and Miscellaneous Essays*)
Present Time, The (*Latter-Day Pamphlets*)
Prinzenraub, The (*Critical and Miscellaneous Essays*)
Promoterism (*Last Words*, 1882)
Repeal of the Union (*Memoirs of Carlyle*)
Reward (*Past and Present*)
Richter, Jean Paul Friedrich (*Critical and Miscellaneous Essays*)
Richter Again, Jean Paul (*Critical and Miscellaneous Essays*)

Romans, Their Character, their Fortune, The (*Centenary Edition*)
St. Edmund (*Past and Present*)
St. Edmundsbury (*Past and Present*)
Schiller (*Critical and Miscellaneous Essays*)
Scott, Sir Walter (*Critical and Miscellaneous Essays*)
Shooting Niagara, and After ? (*Critical and Miscellaneous Essays*)
Signs of the Times, The (*Last Words, 1882; Critical and Miscellaneous Essays*)
Sinking of the 'Vengeur', The (*Critical and Miscellaneous Essays*)
Sir Jabesh Windbag (*Past and Present*)
Spaniards, The (*Centenary Edition*)
Sphinx, The (*Past and Present*)
State of German Literature, The (*Critical and Miscellaneous Essays*)
Stump Orator (*Latter-Day Pamphlets*)
Tale, The (trans.) (*Critical and Miscellaneous Essays*)
Taylor's Historic Survey of German Poetry (*Critical and Miscellaneous Essays*)
Tieck (*Critical and Miscellaneous Essays*)
Trees of Liberty (*Memoirs of Carlyle*)
Twelfth Century (*Past and Present*)
Two Centuries (*Past and Present*)
Two Hundred and Fifty Years Ago (*Critical and Miscellaneous Essays*)
Unworking Aristocracy (*Past and Present*)
Varnhagen von Ense, Letters to (*Critical and Miscellaneous Essays*)
Varnhagen von Ense's Memoirs (*Critical and Miscellaneous Essays*)
Voltaire (*Critical and Miscellaneous Essays*)
Voltaire—the French (*Centenary Edition*)
Werner, Life and Writings of (*Critical and Miscellaneous Essays*)
Working Aristocracy (*Past and Present*)
Wortley, Lady Mary Montagu (*Montaigne; Critical and Miscellaneous Essays*)
Wotton Reinfred: A Romance (*Last Words, 1892*)